My Recipes are for the Birds

A MAIN STREET BOOK
PUBLISHED BY DOUBLEDAY
a division of Bantam Doubleday Dell Publishing Group,
666 Fifth Avenue, New York, New York 10103

MAIN STREET BOOKS, DOUBLEDAY, and the portrayal of a
building with a tree are trademarks of Doubleday, a
division of Bantam Doubleday Dell Publishing Group, Inc.

ISBN 0-385-12634-4
Library of Congress Catalog Card No. 76-023575
Copyright © 1975, 1976 by Irene E. Cosgrove and Ed Cosgrove

22   24   26   25   23

MAIN
STREET
BOOKS

Doubleday

NEW YORK   LONDON   TORONTO
SYDNEY   AUCKLAND

INTRODUCTION

The following recipes have something special for everyone. They will attract and delight the guests at your feeders, and provide the warmth and energy that is needed during the cold winter months.

The Feeding Station

Preparation should be made well in advance of the arrival of your winter guests. The time to begin setting up your feeding station is in the fall when birds begin to gather and migrate. Choose a site that is protected and easy to get to when there is snow on the ground. Three kinds of feeders should be used. Seed dispensers, suet containers and ground feeders.

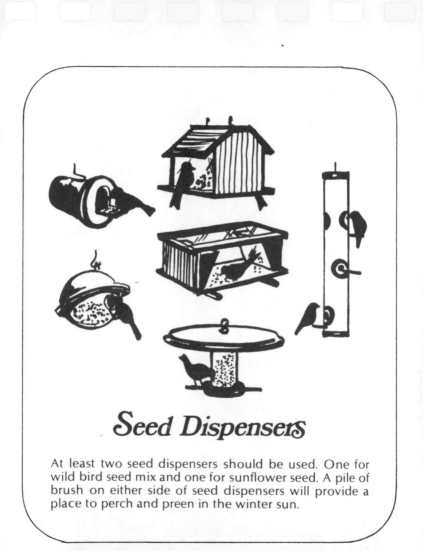

Seed Dispensers

At least two seed dispensers should be used. One for wild bird seed mix and one for sunflower seed. A pile of brush on either side of seed dispensers will provide a place to perch and preen in the winter sun.

Suet Containers

All of your guests will eat suet during the winter for energy and warmth. Several kinds of containers should be used. Netted bags and plastic coated wire baskets are used by small clinging birds. Logs with holes at various points are perfect for woodpeckers and coconut shell halves are used by all.

Ground Feeders

Your feeding station would not be complete without ground feeders. Provide at least two. These can be wooden boxes or plastic containers about 3 inches deep with a few holes drilled through the bottom for drainage. Mourning Doves, Blue Jays and Juncos are ground feeders and they will appreciate this mode of fare. Add grit in the form of Parakeet gravel or clean sand as needed, especially after a rain or snow storm.

Creatures Of Habit

Once you begin feeding, it is most important that you continue through the winter. Check your feeders at least twice a day. As early as possible in the morning and again before dusk. Birds take shelter for the night and do not feed again until dawn.

About The Ingredients

Raw Beef Suet

Suet is very important in providing energy and warmth during the cold winter months. In preparing suet, always put it through a meat grinder before melting it down. It makes a smoother liquid. Reheat to make a solid suet cake.

Sand

Grit is needed to grind and digest the coarse foods that birds eat. Ordinary beach sand will do, or you can provide commercial bird gravel.

Kitchen Scraps

Store your left over cake, donuts, cookies and pie crust in a plastic container with cover. Keep crusts and stale bread in another.

My Own Granola Treat

One cup each of the following: peanut hearts, white millet, wheat germ, crushed dog biscuits, raisins and sunflower seeds. Heat separately $1/2$ cup honey and $1/2$ cup corn oil. Add these to above mixture. Mix well and bake at 375° for 10 minutes. Refrigerate. Granola can be fed as is or combined with suet.

Seeds and Grains

Thistle, millet, sunflower seeds, cracked corn, peanut hearts and wild bird seed can be bought at your local feed shop.

Bluebird Betty

1 Cup sugar	2 Cups flour
1 Cup raisins	1/2 Tsp. baking powder
1/2 Cup shortening	1 Tsp. baking soda
1/2 Cup water	1/3 Cup nutmeats

In a medium size bowl put flour, baking powder and baking soda. Set aside. Boil sugar, raisins, shortening and water for 5 minutes. Add this liquid mixture to the dry ingredients. Mix well. Add nutmeats. Spoon into well greased 8″ x 8″ cake pan. Bake for 20-25 minutes at 350°. Serve in pieces on feeder tray or ground feeder.

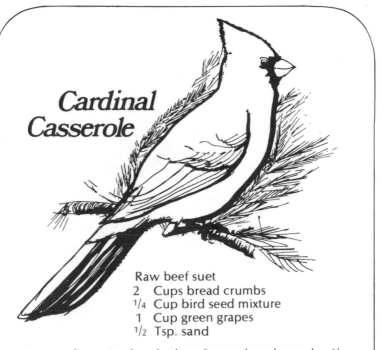

Cardinal Casserole

Raw beef suet
2 Cups bread crumbs
1/4 Cup bird seed mixture
1 Cup green grapes
1/2 Tsp. sand

In a medium size bowl, place 2 cups bread crumbs, 1/4 cup bird seed mixture and 1 cup green grapes, cut in pieces. Set aside. Put beef suet through meat grinder, then into a double boiler to melt. Remove from heat, allow to cool and harden slightly. Reheat and while in liquid form, pour 1 1/2 cups over dry ingredients. Add 1/2 tsp. sand. Mix well with a fork. Turn into a foil loaf size pan, 5" x 3" x 1". Refrigerate until firm. Place on feeder tray.

Chickadee Crunch

Raw beef suet   Pine cones
Sunflower seeds   Millet seed

Put suet through a meat grinder, then melt it down in a double boiler. Set aside to cool and harden slightly. Reheat. Take pine cones with string or wire attached and spoon warm suet over until well coated. Sprinkle immediately with millet, then push sunflower seeds under scales. Spoon warm suet over pine cones again, building up suet and securing sunflower seeds. Refrigerate until firm and hang from tree branches.

Dove Delight

Cracked corn
Peanut hearts
Kitchen scraps

Crushed dog biscuits
Sunflower seeds
Thistle seed

Pour sand and gravel into a plastic container that is 2 to 3 inches deep. To that, add any amount of the ingredients listed above. Replace sand and gravel as often as is necessary, especially after rain or snow.

Finch Fries

Raw beef suet
1 Cup millet
1/2 Cup bread crumbs

1/2 Cup Am. cheese cubed
Sand for grit

Save tuna or cat food size cans. Spoon into 4 of these, a combination of 1 cup millet, 1/2 cup bread crumbs and 1/2 cup Am. cheese cubed. Sprinkle each with a pinch of sand for grit. Put suet through meat grinder, then melt down in a double boiler. Set aside to cool and harden slightly. Reheat. While in liquid form, pour in enough suet to fill tins. Refrigerate to harden. Nail to trees with 6 inch nails. Be sure to tape exposed end of nails to insure a safe perch.

Flicker Fricassee

1 Cup grape nuts	1/4 Tsp. sand
1 Cup raisins	1 1/3 Cups suet
1 Cup peanut hearts	

Into an 8" x 8" cake pan, put grape nuts, raisins, peanut hearts and sand. Set aside. Put suet through a meat grinder, melt down in a double boiler and set aside to cool and harden slightly. Reheat and pour 1 1/3 cups over dry ingredients. Refrigerate until firm, cut in pieces and serve in plastic coated wire basket on tree trunk.

Grosbeak Goolash

1/2 Cup sunflower seeds	1/4 Cup all-bran
1/2 Cup hamster pellets	1/4 Tsp. sand
1/3 Cup dog biscuits	3/4 Cup suet

Put sunflower seeds, hamster pellets, crushed dog biscuits, all-bran and sand into a coconut shell half. Set aside. Put suet through meat grinder and place in double boiler. Melt and set aside to cool and harden slightly. Reheat and while in liquid form pour 3/4 cup over ingredients in coconut shell. Refrigerate to harden.

Jay Jambalaya

Raw beef suet
1/4 Cup meat scraps
1   Cup cornmeal

1/2 Cup bread crumbs
1   Cup peanut hearts
1   Tsp. sand

Save your meat scraps, do not remove fat. Put these through meat grinder and set aside in a medium size bowl. To this add 1 cup cornmeal, 1/2 cup bread crumbs, 1 cup peanut hearts and 1 tsp sand for grit. Cut up suet and put through meat grinder. Place in double boiler, melt, set aside to cool and harden. Reheat and while in liquid form pour 1 cup over dry ingredients. Spoon into suet container and refrigerate until firm.

Junco Jubilee

Raw beef suet
1 Cup cornmeal
3/4 Cup millet

1 Cup cracked corn
1 Tbs. grape jelly
1/2 Tsp. sand

In a loaf size foil pan, put 1 cup cornmeal, 3/4 cup millet and 1 cup cracked corn. Set aside. After putting suet through meat grinder, melt down in a double boiler. Allow to cool and harden slightly. Reheat and stir in 1 tablespoon grape jelly. Pour 1 1/2 cups suet over dry ingredients and add 1/2 tsp. sand for grit. Refrigerate until firm. Serve on feeder tray.

Kinglet Kugel

Raw beef suet
2 Cups bread crumbs
1 Cup grape nuts

1 Cup bird seed
1 Tbs. sugar
1 Tsp. sand for grit

Combine 2 cups bread crumbs, 1 cup grape nuts and 1 cup wild bird seed in medium size bowl and set aside. Put suet through a meat grinder, then melt it down in a double boiler. Remove from heat, allow to cool and harden slightly. Reheat and stir in 1 tbs. sugar. Pour 1 cup suet over dry ingredients, sprinkle with 1 tsp. of sand for grit. Mix well and spoon into a suet feeder, or other suet container you may have.

Mockingbird Muffins

1	Cup cornmeal	3/4	Cup currents
1	Cup flour	1/2	Cup bacon drippings
1	Cup bread crumbs	1/4	Tsp. sand
1/2	Tsp. soda	1	Cup water

Combine cornmeal, flour, grated bread crumbs and soda in a medium size bowl. Add currents and sand. Pour in bacon drippings, water and mix well. Spoon into muffin tins. Bake at 350° for 15 minutes. Serve on feeder tray or impale on branches.

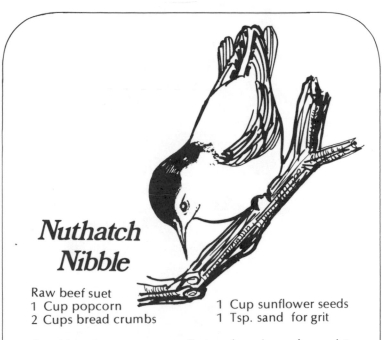

Nuthatch Nibble

Raw beef suet
1 Cup popcorn
2 Cups bread crumbs

1 Cup sunflower seeds
1 Tsp. sand for grit

Combine 1 cup popcorn, 2 cups bread crumbs and 1 cup sunflower seeds in medium size bowl and set aside. After putting suet through meat grinder, melt it down in a double boiler. Remove from heat and allow to harden slightly. Reheat and while in liquid form pour 1½ cups over dry ingredients. Sprinkle with 1 tsp. sand. Stir mixture with a fork until well coated. Turn out onto wax paper, 16 in. Bring paper up around suet, pressing to form a ball. Refrigerate until firm. Place in netted suet bag.

Robin Russe

1	Medium apple	¹/₄	Tsp. sand
¹/₂	Cup raisins	1¹/₂	Cups suet
1	Cup cooked noodles or spaghetti		

In an 8″ x 8″ cake pan, put 1 medium apple, diced, including skin and seeds, ¹/₂ cup raisins, 1 cup cooked noodles or spaghetti and ¹/₄ tsp sand. Set aside. Put suet through a meat grinder, then melt down in a double boiler. Allow suet to cool and harden slightly. Reheat and while in liquid form, pour 1¹/₂ cups over ingredients in pan. Refrigerate to harden, cut into pieces and serve on tray or ground feeder.

Sparrow Stew

Raw beef suet
1½ Cups wild bird seed
1 Cup bread crumbs

1 Cup Graham crackers
½ Tsp. sand

In a medium size bowl, put 1½ cups wild bird seed, 1 cup bread crumbs, 1 cup Graham crackers crumbled and set aside. Put suet through a meat grinder, then melt down in a double boiler. Allow suet to cool and harden slightly. Reheat and while in liquid form pour 1 cup over dry ingredients. Add ½ tsp. sand for grit. Mix well, spoon into a loaf size foil pan 5″ x 3″ x 1″. Refrigerate until firm. Place on feeder tray.

Titmouse *Tidbits*

Raw beef suet
1   Cup dog biscuits
1   Cup kitchen scraps

1   Cup sunflower seeds
2   Tbs. peanut butter
1/2 Tsp. sand

Grind up about 12 dog biscuits in blender and put in medium size bowl. Add 1 cup kitchen scraps, 1 cup sunflower seeds and 2 tbs. peanut butter. Set aside. Put suet through meat grinder. Then melt in double boiler. Remove from heat and allow to cool and harden slightly. Reheat and pour 1 1/2 cups over dry ingredients. Add 1/2 tsp. sand for grit. Mix well and spoon into coconut shell halves. Hang from tree branch.

Waxwing Wedge

Raw beef suet
1   large apple
2   Cups kitchen scraps

3/4 Cup raisins
1   Tsp. sand

Peel and core apple. Put peel through meat grinder and cut apple into small cubes. Place in 8"x 8"cake pan or tin foil container. Add 2 cups kitchen scraps and 3/4 cup raisins that have been steamed in a little water until plump. Put suet through grinder, then melt down in a double boiler. Set aside to cool and harden slightly. Reheat and while in liquid form, pour 1 1/2 cups over fruit and scraps combination. Add 1 tsp. sand. Refrigerate until firm. Cut into wedges to fit your suet feeder.

Woodpecker Wellington

Raw beef suet
1   Cup My Own Granola Treat
1/2 Tsp. sand for grit

Place 1 cup of My Own Granola Treat into an 8 x 8 cake pan and set aside. Put suet through meat grinder, melt it down in a double boiler and remove from heat to cool and harden slightly. Reheat, then pour a cup of liquid suet over granola treat, sprinkle with 1/2 tsp. sand for grit. Refrigerate until firm. Cut into pieces to place in your woodpecker suet feeder.

Wren Wrolls

2	Cups bread crumbs	1	Cup peanut hearts
1/2	Cup coconut	1/2	Tsp. sand
1	Cup raisins	1 1/2	Cups suet

In a large bowl combine 2 cups bread crumbs, 1/2 cup shredded coconut, 1 cup raisins, 1 cup peanut hearts and 1/2 tsp. sand. Put suet through a meat grinder and melt down in a double boiler. Remove from heat and allow to harden slightly. Reheat and while in liquid form pour 1 1/2 cups over dry ingredients. Mix well. Spoon 1/4 of recipe onto a piece of wax paper. Bring sides up around suet, pressing to form a ball or wroll. Refrigerate until firm and serve in a coconut shell.

String Foods

cheese cubes
popcorn
raisins

peanuts in shell
donuts
dried fruit

Return Of Spring

In mid March you may notice fewer birds at your feeders. Tasty sprouts, insects and worms are pushing through the softened ground. Starlings, like armies marching across the still brown lawn, are searching out the natural tidbits. Soon, red winged black birds and robins join the hunt. It is time to stop suet feeding and continue seed feeding until the end of April.

The Nesting Season

The nesting season usually begins in May. This is the time when birds no longer depend upon man for food. Entice them into nesting on your property by providing houses and nesting materials. Houses should be made of natural materials, well ventilated and hung on the shady side of a tree. Nesting materials such as twine, wool and string (in 3" lengths) can be put into the suet containers at this time.